The HIGHER YOU

MINISTER JEREMIAH PRUDE

CONTENTS

INTRODUCTION

The higher you is a regenerated you with a fresh new outlook and a renewed state of mind; it is the upgraded version of yourself. This is the new man who has been made perfect in love, because perfect love casts out all fear. This new man walks in the true knowledge of His creator.

Colossians 3:9-10 (NIV) says:

> *"Do not lie to each other, since you have taken off your old self with its practices and have put on the new self, which is being renewed in knowledge in the image of its Creator."*

This man knows no limits, this man is plugged into the very source of life, itself. The new Adam is full of hope and purpose and he has a definite direction and focus for his life. The new Adam does not live his life aimlessly, but every move he makes, it is with intention. He starts every task with the end in mind. This is what keeps him on track, he is very aware of the *'end game.'* This new man knows who he is, purpose and destiny have awakened him. Purpose has fueled him with the energy to fulfill his dreams. This man has determined to bring his dreams to fruition. The Word says in Proverbs 13:12 (NLT):

> *"Hope deferred makes the heart sick, but a dream fulfilled, is a tree of life."*

This man was made for production. Everything he needs is built within, in order that he fulfills purpose. His eyes are filled with revelation and truth, therefore he is both empowered and enabled to clearly navigate in dark places.

Might I further add, this higher you can only be discovered as you renew your mind. It is as the word says in Romans 12:2 (AMPC):

> *"Do not be conformed to this world (this age, [fashioned after and adapted to its external, superficial customs], but be transformed (changed)*

*by the [entire] renewal of your mind (by its new ideals and its new attitude), so that you may prove [for yourselves] what is the good and acceptable and prefect will of God, even the thing which is good and acceptable and perfect [**In his sight for you**], (emphasis, author).*

Now, this was a mouth full! So, in order to summarize this scripture, let's just say it is important that your mind be able to filter out the influence and noise of outside voices, while at the same time, you manage to follow the promptings of the Holy Spirit. The Holy Spirit is also known as the Spirit of truth, which was given to us, in order that we would be able to be lead into all Truth. We read about this in the epistle of 1 John 2:20, (NIV):

"But you have an anointing from the Holy One, and all of you know the truth."

God's Spirit knows His mind, and the word says we have the mind of Christ. We read in 1Corinthians 2:16 (KJV):

"For who hath known the mind of the Lord, that he may instruct him? But we have the mind of Christ."

This means we know all things by His Spirit, and this in itself, is a powerful reality to grasp, for those of us who are believers. The word tells us in James 1:5 (NIV):

> *"If any of you lacks wisdom, you should ask God, who gives generously to all without finding fault, and it will be given to you."*

Sometimes we must stop straining and simply seek God. As it says in Zechariah 4:6 (NIV):

> *"So he said to me, "This is the word of the Lord to Zerubbabel: 'Not by might nor by power, but by my Spirit,' says the Lord Almighty."*

God's Spirit knows no limits, it has no limitations. In the military we refer to this as a *limifact*, which simply means a limiting factor. If you are connected to the vine, you have no limitations. Remember, the Word of God tells you that you can do all things through Christ who strengthens you.

Chapter 1

SELF-DISCOVERY

elf-Discovery is the greatest adventure you will ever know. It is kind of like your ability to understand Neo in the Matrix. You begin to realize an excitement as you come into the knowledge of who you were created to be. What does the word say in Ephesians 4:23-24, (NLT):

> *"Instead let the Spirit renew your thoughts and attitudes. Put on your new nature, created to be like God— truly righteous and holy.*

However, in order to do this, you must get rid of old thought patterns and ideas you have allowed to permeate the way you think. This will take some work. Remember,

Rome was not built in a day, and your thought pattern was not built over night.

The Bible refers to these thoughts as strongholds. Remember, the Word says as a man thinks in his heart, so is he. Your life moves in the direction of your most dominate thought. Jesus always said to be careful how you hear, let's break this concept down. Say I am in the weight room, lifting weights and a professional body builder comes in and informs me that my lifting technique is wrong. There are a couple of ways in which I may respond to his observation. I may decide to take a negative view of what he said and conclude that this is his attempt to put me down, or I could take a positive stance and determine that his motive was to look out for my best interest. This is where faith comes in, it is up to us to choose to follow the correct voice in our lives. The Word says in Proverbs 16:20, (NIV):

"Whoever gives heed to instruction prospers and blessed is the one who trusts in the Lord." There are many voices in the world, but the voice that really counts is the voice of the Holy Spirit. The Word also says in John 16:13, (NIV):

"But when he, the Spirit of truth, comes, he will guide you into all the truth. He will not speak of his own; he will speak only what he hears and will tell you what is yet to come."

What is truth, some may ask? Truth is whatever God says. The Word says in Isaiah 53:11, (KJV),

> "*Who hath believed our report? and to whom is the arm of the Lord revealed?*"

His report says I am free, and His report says victory! In God's kingdom the results are already in, so we are literally waging a war that is already won. Our only job is to stand firm on what He has already said.

I found myself astonished at what the Apostle Paul wrote, while he was imprisoned. He said he was in chains as an evil doer, but he understood that the Word of God was not bound. We see that Jesus says in John 3:3, (KJV):

> "*Verily, verily, I say unto thee, Except a man be born again, he cannot see the kingdom of God.*"

When you were born again, old things passed away and all things became knew. However, when you bumped your head in the dateless past, you were relegated to a case of severe amnesia and forgot who you really were. Due to that unfortunate head injury, you may need to update your software, because it is out of date and it no longer works.

This is what the Word say in Ecclesiastes 7:29, (NLT):

> *"But I did find this: God created people to be virtuous, but they have each turned to follow their own downward path."*

The real fight is to find the higher version of yourself. This man can only know who he is by means of an intimate relationship with the one who made him. The one who cares for him.

How do you act toward someone you believe does not have your best interest at heart? You are probably always watching them out of the corner of your eye, because you know you can never really trust them. Well, we certainly know that is not the case with God. What was God's original intention for your life? We sometimes need God to remind us, in His own words, of His intentions toward us. Therefore, it says in the word in Jeremiah 29:11, (NIV):

> *"For I know the plans I have for you, declares the Lord, plans to prosper you and not to harm you, plans to give you hope and a future."*

God's Word is so good because He always tells us the truth. You see, the truth sounds like fiction when you live in a world that is filled with lies and deception. Therefore, you must constantly renew your mind by the washing of the water of the Word, this serves to ensure you will not be deceived. The Word says in Hebrews 9:14, (KJV),

"...how much more shall the blood of Christ, who through the eternal Spirit offered himself without spot to God, purge your conscience from dead works to serve the living God?"

Instead of being self-conscious, you must learn how to be God-concise. Your self-worth does not come from you, it comes from the one who made you. Just like it is only the manufacturer of the vehicle who knows the true value of the vehicle, because he or she understands the true essence of the vehicle in it's entirety. The Word of God says in Genesis 1:27, (KJV):

"So God created man in his own image, in the image of God created he him; male and female he created he them."

By now we are all familiar with the meaning of 'DNA,' your DNA is your genetic code. This genetic code, which has been passed down from your parents, tells us all about you. I find this fascinating. We may witness a child with behavior that is exactly like his father's and yet, this child may have never met his father in person before. You see the Word says that God knew you before you were even formed in your mother's womb. If this is the case, then He has known you longer than anyone else, self included. Therefore, the Word says in Psalms 139:13 - 16, (NLT):

> *"You made all the delicate, inner parts of my body and knit me together in my mother's womb. Thank you for making me so wonderfully complex! Your workmanship is marvelous -how well I know it. You watched me as I was being formed in utter seclusion, as I was woven together in the dark womb. You saw me before I was born. Every day of my life was recorded in your book. Every moment was laid out before a single day had passed."*

Now this is what I call a selah moment! This means you are to pause and give this some serious thought. You see, we have been created for good works. The Word says in Ephesians 2:20, (NLT):

> *"For we are God's masterpiece. He has created us anew in Christ Jesus, so we can do the good things he planned for us long ago.*

Now this excites me! I have to say Hallelujah! You see, the reason you are here is because you already had a purpose before your parents even thought about hooking up; you were already in the mind of God. We must change our perspective; you see, it is God who declares the end at the beginning. The reason He does this is because He already knows the end. Therefore, we can have great confidence in what He has to say which concerns us. The Word says that He will perfect all those things that concern you. It says in Psalms 138:8, (ESV):

> *"The Lord will fulfill his purpose for me; your steadfast love, O Lord, endures forever. Do not forsake the work of Your hands."*

God is too good to leave you where he found you. Jesus said that He came to seek for that, which was lost. Now imagine that. God is looking for you, and this why he said, "Adam where are you?" The key word here is "You." You must learn to personalize the Word of God. You see Jesus is God's work personified. This means He is the Living Word, God With Us, Emmanuel, Hallelujah! Here, again, is another reason I find myself excited, it is because the Word was made flesh and dwelt among us. You see the Lord went low, in order for us to go high. The Word tells us in Philippians 2:7, (KJV):

> "...but made Himself of no reputation, and took upon him the form of a servant, and was made in the likeness of men...."

Now, just imagine being the creator of the universe, and making a decision to be subject to the creation that you actually created, this had to be a very humbling experience. This is why the Lord hates a proud look, this is why He resists the proud, but He gives grace to the humble. He did all of this to redeem us back to Himself and to take us high into the heavens with Him. The Word says in Ephesians 2:6 *(KJV)*:

> "And hath raised us up together and made us sit together in heavenly places in Christ Jesus."

You see in Him is life and this life is the light of all men, once you have made a decision to seek life, you then become what you seek after. Therefore, Jesus said if any man wants to follow Me, he must first deny himself and then pick up his cross and follow Me. You need to understand, it is the higher version of yourself that is hidden in Christ. The Word tells us that we died and were baptized and buried with Him in death. It says in Romans 6:4, (NIV):

> *"We were therefore buried with him through baptism into death in order that, just as Christ was raised from the dead through the glory of the Father, we too may live a new life."*

The key word here is 'NEW' life.

Chapter 2

SELF-ACTUALIZATION

elf-Actualization...let us take a look at one of it's definitions:

What occurs when a person can take full advantage of his or her talents, while being mindful of his or her limitations.

Now that you have discovered this higher version of yourself, it is now time to live and act like, this higher version of yourself. This is why the Word says in Ephesians 5:14, (NIV):

"Wake up, sleeper, rise from the dead, and Christ will shine on you."

You are now woke, and it is time for you to get acquainted with the higher you. It is as if you went under for a while; kind of like being under anesthesia. The Lord had to give you a new spirit and a new heart. Now, your eyes are open and you can see clearly, Hallelujah! You are a son now, the Word says in 1 John 3:1, (NIV):

> *"See what great love the* Father *has lavished on us, that we should be called the children of God!* *And that is what we are! The reason the world does not know us is that it did not know him."*

The Higher you is no longer looking for acceptance from others, because you now realize that you are connected to your Creator. You now realize that your footsteps are ordered by the Lord, and you no longer need to question who you are, because you now know who you are. The Word says, in Ephesians 1:6, (KJV):

> *"To the praise of the glory of his grace, wherein he had made us accepted in the beloved.*

You must remember, however, that this new person must be cultivated and developed. I once heard a preacher say that your mind is like a garden. You must feed off of whatever you have planted there. So, with this in mind, we must do what it says in the Word. We must be constantly renewed in the spirit of our minds, as it says in Ephesians 4:23, (AMP):

> "...and be continually renewed in the spirt of your mind [having a fresh, untarnished mental and spiritual attitude]...."

Scripturally, I now see that this is a continuous process, this is not a 'one and done' type of deal. As you know, the battlefield is the mind, therefore we must always be alert. The Word of God tells us that the devil roams around like a lion seeking whom he may devour and Jesus told us to watch, as well as pray; in other words, we must be cognizant of what is going on around us at all times. In the military we refer to this as *situational awareness.* We must remember that the battle that is being waged is not a physical battle but a spiritual one. Trust me, this is hard to comprehend at times. However, we must remember that everything first happens in the spiritual realm, before it hits the physical realm. That is why we must be sober-minded at all times, so that we can see straight. I have already said to you that the enemy is always in an attempt to slip up on you, but it is worth repeating again, we find this warning in 1Peter 5:8-9, (NIV):

"Be alert and of sober mind. Your enemy the devil prowls around like a roaring lion looking for someone to devour.

Remember, the first Adam was just a man, but the second Adam is the Lord from heaven. Jesus is called the second Adam in many translations of the Bible. In order to experience the higher you, the old you must be crucified with its affections and lusts. I will compare this to the caterpillar's metamorphoses into a butterfly. Obviously, a transformation has taken place. The Word says in Romans 6:6, (NLT):

"We know that our old sinful selves were crucified with Christ so that sin might lose its power in our lives."

This new man is an entirely different race of mankind. Jesus said that the flesh profits nothing, but it is the spirit that gives life. Jesus also said in Matt 10:39, (NIV):

"Whoever finds his life will lose it and whoever loses his life for My sake will find it.

Hallelujah! The key comment here is *for My sake.* When you dedicate your life to the Lord, you no longer belong to yourself, because you were bought with a price. Therefore, it is no longer about you, you are now part of a different kingdom. Just like the fact that Christ said that the Son of man, did not come to be served, but to serve. In God's kingdom the way up, is down, first. Jesus, said that a seed abides alone, unless it at least goes into the ground and dies first, then after it's death, it produces many seeds. This new experience to find the higher you can be scary at first, but do not worry, the Lord is with you. He promised to never leave you nor forsake you. Remember, you have been called for such a time as this. Jesus is the pioneer of this new life. As it says in the Word in 1Corinthians 15:22-23, (NIV):

> *"For as in Adam all die, so in Christ all will be made alive. But each in his turn: Christ the first fruits; then, when he comes, those who belong to him."*

You see Christ is the first born of the dead. The Word calls Him the first born among many brethren. You see, He tasted death first, in order to bring us to life. Hallelujah! This really causes me to get excited, because God is good! The Word says taste and see that the Lord is good. You see Jesus is not the only begotten Son of God anymore; we too, are also begotten of God. Before you declare this to be blasphemy, let me take you on this journey with me and prove it by the Word. It says in 1Peter 1:3, (ASV):

> *"Blessed be the God and Father of our Lord Jesus Christ, who according to his great mercy begat us again unto a living hope by the resurrection of Jesus Christ from the dead."*

Now, I have to say *'Selah'*! This means pause and calmly think about that. Hallelujah! This also gets me excited! You see, the Gospel is called, *"the good news."* You see man fell from a lofty state of being to a low estate of existence. When you are in a fallen state you do not know where true north is anymore, therefore you need guidance. As it says in Romans 1:28, (NIV): *"Furthermore, just as they did not think it worthwhile to retain the knowledge of God, so God gave them over to a depraved mind, so that they do what not ought to be done."*

In this world, there is a catastrophic level of severe identity crisis among men and women. This is why you see men lying with men, and women lying with women. The Word said that God gave them over to their depraved mind to dishonor themselves. Now it is one thing to dishonor someone else, but to dishonor yourself, this is a whole other level of lowliness. When you lose respect for yourself, it only stands to reason that you will not respect anyone outside of yourself.

I can remember growing up in the hood, if some 'so called person' disrespected you, that was reason enough to fight them; no matter the situation. You see man was made to reflect the glory of God, and we were made in His image and likeness. The Lord God is a ruler, so of course the acorn does not fall far from the Oak. However, in order to be one to rule, you must first conquer and rule yourself. The Word says in Proverbs 16:32, (NLT):

> *"Better to be patient than powerful; better to have self-control than to conquer a city."*

The higher you is now back in tune with his redeemed spirit-man. The Word says in Romans 8:6 – 10, (NLT):

> *"So letting your sinful nature control your mind leads to death. But letting the Spirit control your mind leads to life and peace. For the sinful nature is always hostile to God. It never did obey God's laws, and it never will. That's why those who are still under the control of their sinful nature God can never please God. But you are not controlled by your sinful nature. You are controlled by the Spirit of God living in you. (And remember that those who do not have the*

Spirit of Christ living in them do not belong to him at all.) And Christ lives within you, so even though your body will die because of sin, the Spirt gives you life because you have been made right with God."

Many people, via their choices, are self-banished from the life of God, because of the ignorance that is in them. When the purpose or identity of a thing or person is lost, then abuse is inevitable. When you make a decision to make a purchase of an item, you first read the manufacturer's instructions for it's maximum use. God's Word is his precepts, laws, and principles. Whenever you operate by these laws, you are operating like God, Himself. You see Jesus is, therefore, referred to as the God-man, because He and His Father's nature are the same. Therefore, Jesus always said if you have seen Me, you have seen the Father. David asked himself in Psalms 8:4 – 6, (KJV):

"What is man, that thou are mindful of him? And the son of man, that thou visitest him? For thou have made him a little lower than the angels and hast crowned him with glory and honor, thou made him to have dominion over

the works of thy hand; thou has put all things under him feet."

Let's please understand that this verse, with regard to angels, is actually Elohim, Himself and not angels. This is the only position it can be if angels are to minister to us.

We have now arrived to the point in this book, where you may want to ask the question, what happened? In a nutshell, we could say that Jesus, the second Adam came to reverse the curse of the first Adam. I like to call this, "...*When the empire strikes back, the return of the Jedi, (that is Jesus)."*

Remember, it was prophesied way back in Genesis 3:15 (NIV):

> *"And I will put enmity between you and the woman, and between your offspring and hers; he will crush your head, and you will strike his heel."*

You see Christ is the *'promised seed,'* however, we are joint heirs with Christ, so we share in His inheritance, as rightful heirs with Him. You see when you are awakened to the higher you, then you realize that you have everything you need to succeed. The Word tells us that He has already given us all things that pertain to life and godliness. Our job is to manifest this for the world to see. You see the Word says in Proverbs 22:4, (NIV):

"Humility is the fear of the LORD, its wages are riches and honor and life."

Wow, now this Scripture is amazing to me, because it talks about the benefits I have just as the SON. Yes, I said benefits. You have inherited a Kingdom and you do not even know it. What if I told you that you came into an inheritance worth a billion dollars? You would be so excited to learn about your new status in life. I bet you would poke your chest out and walk with some pep in your step, (you would have what I call that "Holy Swag"). Like my homeboy told me, "He said Jesus is the *'mackaville'* of my soul."

Chapter 3

SON'S IMAGE

The Son's image. Now that you bear the image of the Son, you have full rights and privileges. The Word says in John 1:11-13, (NIV):

"He came to that which was his own, but his own did not receive him. Yet to all who did receive him, to those who believed in his name, he gave the right to become children of God, children born not of natural descent, nor of human decision or a husband's will, but born of God." **Selah***!*

(author's emphasis).

Pause and calmy think about that. You have a blessed heritage now, and it does not matter what kind of family you came from, you have been adopted into a new family. You are truly a King's kid, and you are an extension of His Lordship. Now His Kingdom will be coming through you, because it is within you. You see, you were created to bring glory to God. This is why the Word says in Luke 12:32, (NIV):

> *"Do not be afraid, little flock, for your Father has been pleased to give you the kingdom."*

Hallelujah! Now the kingdom is wherever a king decides to take up his dominion and extend his rule. Therefore, it says in the Word, in Matthew 6:10, (KJV):

> *"Thy Kingdom come, Thy will be done in earth as it is in heaven."*

He wants us to know that this is how we should always pray. God's will is simply for you to be just like Him. Just like it says in Ephesians 5:1, (NLT):

> *"Imitate God, therefore, in everything you do, because you are his dear children."*

You see the higher you is the new man, who is now woke. The Lord wants to open your eyes and give you insight instead of eyesight. You can see only so much with your naked eye because its scope is limited. Therefore, Jesus told the Pharisees that He called them blind because they claimed to be able to see. He said follow Me and you will not stumble in the darkness. Jesus said in John 31-32, (NIV):

> *"If you hold to my teaching, you are really my disciples. Then you will know the truth, and the truth will set you free."*

You see the truth is a person, and in order to know a person, you must be well acquainted with the person. This means you must take time to learn this person's ways and disposition by time spent with them. Jesus said in John 15:5, (NIV), *"I am the vine, and you are the branches. If you remain in me and I in you, you will bear much fruit; apart from me you can do nothing.* You see you have been given grace and glory; you have received a kingdom that cannot be shaken, as it says in Hebrews 12:28-29, (NIV):

> *"Therefore since we are receiving a kingdom that cannot be shaken, let us be thankful, and so*

worship God acceptably with reverence and awe
for our "God is a consuming fire."

It is the higher you that is now able to access heaven. Now that is some powerful stuff. Jesus said, "I will give you the keys to the kingdom of heaven."

Chapter 4

THINKING PATTERNS

Thinking patterns - you know the olde saying, "You are what you eat." This also holds true for the mind, you are what you think! There is a saying that goes like this, 'There is the man who thinks he can, and there is one who thinks he can't; they are both right!' Proverbs 23:7, (KJV), says,

"For as he thinketh in his heart so is he."

You actually become more of the sum total of thought's you allow to dominate your psyche. Your psyche is where the sub-conscious dwells.

The Lord operates in the faith realm and as His offspring, so should we. If we are really His children, we are supposed to operate the same way. People speak what they believe. This is why the Word says in Romans 10:9 -11, (NIV):

> *"If you declare with your mouth "Jesus is Lord," and believe in your heart that God raised him from the dead, you will be saved. For it is with your heart that you believe and are justified, and it is with your mouth that you profess your faith and are saved."*

The key word in this Scriptural verse is, 'You.' You have the power. The same power that raised Christ from the dead is also at work in you, especially for those who believe. The Word tells us that all things are possible to those who believe, but the Word did not say it was to those who believed in Jesus Christ. You see God knows the power of belief, because he understands the human spirit. Why do you think it is that man can still accomplish such extraordinary things, while he is even in a fallen state? If man can do this in a fallen state, then just imagine for a moment the power of a redeemed spirit, that would be 'YOU!' It says in the Word, in Hebrews 12:23, (KJV):

> *"To the great assembly and the church of the firstborn, which are written in heaven, and to*

God the Judge of all, and to the spirts of just men
made perfect."

You see, you have already been made perfect in the eye's of God.

You must take hold of the reins of authority that have already been given to you, and in order to take authority, you must take action. I sincerely believe that believers have truly forgotten that the Bible is a book that is more about action, as opposed to just mere words. The Word says that the doers of the Word will be justified. I remember this old preacher who would always say, "...don't just sit there, do something." David said in Psalms 144:1, (KJV):

"Blessed be the Lord which teacheth my hands to
war, and my fingers to fight."

You see the Lord is a man of war, and we are His children, so like father like son. We must be a people that are willing to fight for what we want. The Lord never promised that it would be an easy road. He just promised that He would never leave us or forsake us. He told us He would be with us in trouble. It says in Psalms 91:15, (NIV):

"He will call on me, and I will answer him; I will be with him in trouble, I will deliver him and honor him."

Have any of you ever been in any serious trouble? I have, but we will not get into any of those details in this book. However, the point is, the Lord is with you because you are His child. This is powerful because, you see, the Most High is a parent. This means that we have divine protection because we are connected to Him. Let's remember, it is possible for you to sit outside of that protection, but He is the only one that has the jurisdiction over us, and operates it. Jurisdiction means the territory or sphere of activity by which the legal authority of a court or other institution extends. You see, this is the good news for most of us, because how many people have ever stepped outside of His will? You see, we belong to a different kingdom. You remember, Jesus said, "My Kingdom is not of this world." This kingdom we have received, is a kingdom that can never be shaken. Hallelujah! This just makes me want to dance and shout. Remember they asked Jesus how to pray and he told them, to pray,

"Thy kingdom come thy will be done on earth as it in heaven." (Matthew 6:10, KJV).

You see, we are supposed to be an extension of His rule in heaven. Remember, a king must have a kingdom, this is what makes him a king. He must have dominion over the area that he rules. In the military we would call this your (*AOR*), which simply means your '*area of responsibility*.' A lion is called the King of the jungle, because he rules his domain. You see, therefore, Jesus is called the King of kings and Lord of lords. In order to walk in authority, you must believe that YOU possess it. Remember, the Word says in Mark 9:23, (NKJV):

> *"Jesus said to him, If you can believe, all things are possible to him who believes."*

Your actions must line up with your beliefs. You are a hidden treasure, a divine seed. Do not bury your treasure. Remember, you are a seed. The Word says that a seed abides alone unless it goes into the ground and dies. Do not regret your past and all of the mistakes you have made. God had to kill you in order for you to experience the higher you. Under ground is a very dark and obscure place. It is very lonely at times. You may even feel like God has forsaken you in a season such as this. However, this is the place where you are being shaped and molded into who you are destined to be. Remember, the Word says in Matthew 10:39, (KJV):

"He that findeth his life shall lose it: and he that loseth his life for my sake shall find it."

You see, whatever you may be suffering now, it is only so that you will be prepared for the greater glory to be revealed in you. Like it says in Romans 8:18, (Amp):

"[But what of that?] For I consider that the sufferings of this present time (this present life) are not worth being compared with the glory that is about to be revealed to US and in US and for US and conferred on US!" (Emphasis, author).

Every seed produces after its own kind. The pain you endure is tailor made for you and your destiny. No man or women has ever walked in your footsteps, because your path has been ordained before the foundations of the world.

Chapter 5

SONSHIP

The world is waiting for the manifestation of the Sons of God. The Word says in Daniel 11:32, (KJV):

"And such as do wickedly against the covenant shall he corrupt by flatteries: **but the people that do know their God shall be strong, and do exploits.***"* (Emphasis, author).

Just think about Star Wars how they were always exploring other planets. The higher you, that has been redeemed, is back and connected to the vine of life. Now are you ready for takeoff? You are now part of another kingdom that has different dimensions. You are just what the doctor ordered. It is time for you to speak those things that be not as though they were. You are the chosen one. It is time to begin your journey. As you begin your journey, you will need lamp posts along the way. This is the only way you will know that you are on the right track. There will always be a voice behind you telling you the direction in which you should go. As it says in the Word, in Isaiah 30:21, (NIV):

> *"Whether you turn to the right or to the left, your ears will hear a voice behind you, saying, "This is the way, walk in it."*

Always know that you are never alone in your journey. Sonship can never be lost, but it can be squandered. Like it says in the Word, in John 8:35, (NIV):

> *"Now a slave has no permanent place in the family, but a son belongs to it forever."*

You must show up, because the world is waiting for your appearance; and when you are free, you give others the right to become free, as well. The Bible refers to it as the glorious freedom of the sons of God. What does glorious freedom mean or look like? When I think of glorious freedom, I think of an eagle soaring the sky, carefree. Not burdened down with the thoughts of limitations or failure. I have to quote the rapper, Jay-z, when he says in one of the verses of his rap, "What would you do if you knew you could not fail?" That rap verse speaks volumes to me. You see failure is a state of mind not a state of being.

For example, I used to be on the wrestling team, back in the day. I participated in a big tournament; I mean this event was huge. I considered myself to be a fairly good wrestler at the time. I had all of the visible qualities, the speed, the strength, and the technique. However, the biggest quality that I believe I possessed was determination. If memory serves me correctly, it was in the beginning of the tournament, I had lost at least three matches in a row. The irony of it, is my coach could not believe that I had lost those matches, because I wrestled so hard all of the time. However, I never had time to sulk over it because I had to get ready for the next match. You see, in my mind I was never defeated, because I knew I had given my best in each match. Also, understand that each time you lose you get put into a lower bracket. So finally, I won my fourth match, because my coach said that I simply out-worked the other guy. Somehow, I ended up in this lower bracket of guys with defeated spirits, but mine was never defeated. So, finally I had my last match of the tournament, I remember looking across the mat at my opponent, and I could see the defeat in his eyes. My coach told me to go out there and pin him, so we could go home, and that is exactly what I did in about 45 seconds. Another example I like to use is Thomas Edison, the great inventor. When they asked him how did it feel to have failed so many times before being successful, he simply responded by saying, "I have not failed, I have just found 10,000 ways that do not work." You see, it is all about how you view yourself. When it comes down to it, other's perception of you really does not matter. I know that It has been said that perception is reality, but I ask the question whose reality is it, their's or your's? You see everybody has preconceived notions, but this has nothing to do with who you are. In John 8:14, (NIV):

> Jesus answered, *"Even if I testify on my own behalf, my testimony is valid, for I know where I came from and where I am going. But you have no idea where I come from or where I am going."*

It is up to you to follow the beat of your own drum and stay on course. You must know who YOU are, as well as whose YOU are, and do not forget, you must also know where YOU are going.

Chapter 6

THE POWER OF RIGHT BELIEVING

ou are what you think. Henry Ford said, the man that thinks he can and the man that thinks he cannot they are both right. You must clear your mind on a daily basis of self-defeating thoughts. Your value is not based on your actions or your performance, but on who you belong to. You have already been approved by the Most High. This means that you have the highest endorsement there is. You must clean your spirit from the impure water, which leads to impure thoughts. Your mind is like a garden, you must eat off of what you have planted there. You must also water your garden daily with both the Word of God and words of affirmation. Consider writing yourself a confession of faith and reciting it daily.

Chapter 7

DEFINE YOURSELF

*Y*ou must see yourself as an overcomer rather than an *'undergoer.'* I once heard it said that the world is as you see it. Jesus said in John16:33, (KJV):

"These things I have spoken unto you, that in me ye might have peace. In the world ye shall have tribulation: but be of good cheer; I have overcome the world."

You can either be a victim or victor. The Word says in 2 Corinthians 2:14, (NLT):

"But thank God! He has made us his captives and continues to lead us along in Christ's triumphal

procession. Now he uses us to spread the knowl-
edge of Christ everywhere, like a sweet perfume."

Hallelujah!! That makes me want to shout and scream. You see, YOU are the main character in this story and are the victor because the Lord said YOU are. Your mouth will line up with your thoughts. This means you will speak what you think. The Word says in Luke 6:45, (NLT):

"A good person produces good things from the treasury of a good heart, and an evil person produces evil things from the treasury of an evil heart."

What you say flows from what is in your heart. You must keep a positive self-image, in order to do this, you must only speak what is true. Some might ask what is truth? Well, the truth is whatever God says and particularly what He says about YOU. The Word tells us that man shall not live by bread alone but by every word that proceeds out of the mouth of God. Jesus said the words that He spoke were spirit and life. Your spirit is in complete alignment with the Lord, but it is your soul that must be bought into submission. David says in Psalms 25:1, (KJV):

"Unto thee, O Lord, I life up my soul."

In order to lift your soul; you must surrender your will. The Hebrew word for soul is, (nephesh), in the Greek. This word can be translated, as soul, life, creature, appetite, desire, emotion, passion, or person. This is when the supernatural life will infuse your body and take over, then Christ, the hope of Glory, and king of Glory will swallow up your natural life. God has prepared a place for you, and that place is in Him. The Apostle Paul said in Acts 17:28, (KJV):

> *"For in him we live and move and have our being, as some of your poets have said, we are his offspring."*

You must continue to dig deeper into yourself to find the God-given talents that lie dormant within you. You are a gift to the world, and you must see yourself as such. The Bible says in Proverbs 18:16, (KJV):

> *"A man's gift maketh room for him, and bringeth him before great men."*

Doors will open for you if you begin to exercise your gift, no matter what that gift is. You cannot bury your talent and expect to receive a harvest. The word says in Matthew 5:15, (KJV):

> *"Neither do people light a candle and put it under a bushel."*

Instead, a lamp is placed on a stand, where it gives light to everyone in the house. Your playing small does not benefit others. You see, light brings revelation, and revelation brings understanding. Revelation is simply the unveiling of knowledge. You can never really understand who you were created to be unless God gives you the revelation of who you are, and this comes strictly by insight not eyesight.

Chapter 8

VISONARY

ou must a have vision for your life. Jesus said, "Follow Me, and you will not stumble in the darkness." When you have a vision for your life, it ushers in purpose, and purpose gives you direction. You see, everything about you is based on your purpose. I know for me, personally, every job career assessment I ever did, said that I was earmarked to become a guidance counselor or a teacher; this assessment certainly falls in line with who I am. Vision brings clarity to your life, especially when things do not appear to be going the way you want them to. The Word say in Proverbs 29:18, (KJV):

"Where there is no vision, the people perish: But he that keepeth the law, happy is he."

It is your vision that keeps you alive and gives you hope, when you sometimes find that you become weary in well doing. There is reward at the end of the rainbow, this is why the Lord put the rainbow in the sky after the flood; as a sign to signify to humanity that he would never destroy the earth again by water. You must write down your personal vision for your life. This should be a guidepost for your life, and every decision you make, going forward, should be in line with your vision. One of my former pastors would say you are either gaining ground or losing ground. Remember, it is never too late to gain the ground you may have lost because of disobedience, unbelief, or just being lost. I like to call Jesus, the equalizer. He not only knows how to deliver you in one day, but He brings you up to speed, and gives you a date with your destiny. All I can say is, Hallelujah! God is awesome. Remember, you are never alone in your journey. Remember, God is for you.

Chapter 9

MISSIONARY

*A*fter you write down your vision, you must become a missionary. To quote the famous actor, Denzel Washington, "Dreams are just dreaming without goals." I want to share with you an acronym that I learned while in military-leadership school. It is S M A R T. Your goals need to be SMART. Let's break down each letter:

S – Specific - What is your objective and how will you achieve it?

M – Measurable - How do you gauge that you are getting close to your objective or goal?

A – Attainable - Is your goal practical enough for the resources you have at your deposal?

R – Realistic - Is your goal sensible and can it be done?

T – Timely - Finally, you need a timeline for when the goal/goals will be achieved.

Never have so much pride, that it hinders your ability to seek advice. Consider this passage of Scripture in Luke 14:31, (NLT):

"Or what king would go to war against another king without first sitting down with his counselors to discuss whether his army of 10,000 could defeat the 20,000 soldiers marching against him."

Let me give you another example. If you planned to run in a marathon, you would need to prepare. First, you would probably set-in-stone, a projected date of when you would like to run the marathon. Next, you would probably make yourself a running schedule, by which to train. You would certainly increase your miles, gradually, as your body would build in endurance. I have learned in my life that it is far easier to do things in a systematic way, this just keeps one on track. Lastly, be mindful of distractions and never allow them to deter you from your goals. Remember, there will always be naysayers, lining the path of your journey. Jesus said in Luke 6:26, (TPT): "*What sorrows await those of you who are always honored and lauded by others. For that's how your forefathers treated every other false prophet.*"

You must follow the beat of your own drum. Everyone is not going to be a on your team, You must learn to go at it alone, sometimes.

Chapter 10

TAKE AIM

*Y*ou can not hit a target you have not aimed for. This statement may seem obvious to you, but for many, it is not. You must have a target to aim for, otherwise, how will you know if you missed it? I believe that one door serves to open another. I believe that God reveals His plans for us as we act. The Word says in James 2:17-19, (NKJV):

> *"Thus also faith by itself, if it does not have works, is dead, But someone will say, "You have faith, and I have works, Show me your faith without your works, and I will show you my faith by my works."*

My father always says that a man will be remembered by

what he has built; this speaks to legacy. It takes faith to leave a legacy. God told Abraham to leave his own country and go to a land that He would show him. Wow! can you imagine leaving your home country to travel to a land that will be shown to you, after the fact? Most people are afraid to move to another city or state simply because it is unfamiliar territory. Faith is an action word, faith without corresponding action is dead. In order to live by faith, you must act, The Lord spoke the world into existence. He said, "Let there be light and there was." The Word says in 2 Corinthians 4:13, (NIV):

"It is written: *"I believed therefore I have spoken."* Since we have that same spirit of faith, we also believe and therefore speak."

Remember, that life and death are in the power of the tongue. You will have what you speak. Out of the abundance of the heart the mouth speaks. In other words, you speak what is in your heart. That is what the Word says in Proverbs 4:23, (NIV):

"Above all else, guard your heart, for everything you do flows from it."

How do you guard your heart? You guard your heart by mediating on the Word, and at he same time you must protect your eye gate and ear gate. Remember, faith comes by hearing. Who and what do you listen to? You must constantly cast down vain imaginations, as it says in the word in 2 Corinthians 10:5, (TPT):

> *"We can demolish every deceptive fantasy that opposes God and break through every arrogant attitude that is raised up in defiance of the true knowledge of God, We capture like prisoners of war, every thought and insist that It bow in obedience to the Anointed one."*

Chapter 11

FIRE

The first step to any mission begins with the first step. You must start to walk toward your goals. If anyone has ever been on the shooting range, you know that once you take aim, the first thing they tell you to do is, "fire." Some things can only be learned while you are in motion. It is like what the Word says in Matthew 7:24-27, (NIV):

> "*Therefore everyone who hears these words of mine and puts them into practice*, is like a *wise man who built his house on the rock, The rain came down, the streams rose, and the winds blew, yet it did not fall, because it had its foundation on the rock.*"

There is great power in movement. You must be a doer of your own vision, this is how your words become flesh; you must put action behind them. Even the kingdom of God is not in word only, but it is also in deed.

Chapter 12

ADJUST YOUR SIGHTS

*N*ever be afraid to adjust your sights. This is a term that is used on the shooting range when you continue to miss the target. The instructor will come over to you and instruct you to turn your gauge on your weapon a few clicks to the left or right. Do not become frustrated if you do not hit your target right away; sometimes small adjustments make a big difference. Learn to fall in love with the process, everything has a process. Even Jesus had to go through a process in order that He would become who He was destined to be. You see, time is really an illusion, a created thing. God uses time to perfect His purposes concerning you. Stay on your path and continue to adjust your sights along the way. Have you ever used binoculars? A pair of good ones will have a button on them, which will allow you to adjust the vision, so as to see things more clearly. The Word says in Habakkuk 2:2, (KJV):

> *"And the answered me, and said, write the vision, and make it plain upon tables, that he may run that readeth it."*

You see, if you do not know where you are going, you will probably end up some place else. Continue to run with purpose and remember, this is not a race, but a marathon. Remember to keep in step with your own vision, even if you are helping someone else to fulfill their's.

Chapter 13

FINISH THE COURSE

*P*aul said in 2 Timothy 4:7, (KJV):

"I have fought the good fight, I have finished MY COURSE, I have kept the faith." (author's emphasis).

The only course you must finish is your's. My Uncle Stevie told me to never measure myself by the size of another man's coat. Your mantle has been uniquely tailor-made for you. It is especially important to never compare yourself to another man, because you are the one that has been called to a particular people, for a specific purpose. You are prefect for your purpose. It is called *purpose by design*. Like the Lord told Jeremiah, He said,

"I knew you before I formed you in your mother's womb...." (Jeremiah 1;5, NLT).

Therefore, remember, you must follow the paths that have already been etched out for you, this is your course. It says in Psalms 139:16, (NLT):

> *"You saw me before I was born. Every day of my life was recorded in your book. Every single moment was laid out before a single day had passed."*

Hallelujah! This makes me want to scream and shout! In the streets they say stick to the *G-code,* but all you have to do is stick to the GOD CODE. Your steps have been ordained before the foundation of the world. It is now your time, run your race and finish your course.